WHO KEPT THE KEYS?

GoFundMe collapsed. The hat came back empty.

And believe it or not... they were surprised.

By Emory I. Gary Jr.

Simple Options Publishing Presents

The Simple Options Series

Who Kept the Keys?

GoFundMe collapsed.

The hat came back empty.

And believe it or not...

thry were surprised.

Other Books in the Simple Options Series Include:

• Life Insurance Sopranos Style — The Consigliere's Obituary Packet

• Pizza & Proverbs — Lessons Served Hot

• The Plan B Method — When "Later" Isn't an Option

• Invisible Assets — The Wealth You Can't See

• The Keys Left Behind — Discovery Workbook

Simple Options Publishing

Atlanta, Georgia

www.SimpleOptions4.Life

Intangible Assets / Simple Options Series — Copyright © 2025 by Emory I. Gary Jr.

Who Kept the Keys?

Intangible Assets / Simple Options Series — Copyright © 2025 by Emory I. Gary Jr.

Who Kept the Keys?

Copyright © 2025 by Emory I. Gary Jr.

All rights reserved. No part of this book may be reproduced, stored in a retrieval system, or transmitted in any form or by any means—electronic, mechanical, photocopying, recording, or otherwise—without prior written permission of the author, except in the case of brief quotations embodied in critical reviews and certain other noncommercial uses permitted by copyright law.

ISBN: 979-8-9934390-0-6

This book is a work of nonfiction presented in a parable style. Names, characters, places, and incidents are either products of the author's imagination or are used fictitiously. Any resemblance to actual persons, living or dead, or actual events is purely coincidental.

Printed in the United States of America.

First Edition

Self-Published by Emory I. Gary Jr.

Atlanta, Georgia

Intangible Assets / Simple Options Series — Copyright © 2025 by Emory I. Gary Jr.

Who Kept the Keys?

Intangible Assets / Simple Options Series — Copyright © 2025 by Emory I. Gary Jr.

Dedication

For those who have ever been left holding everything.

May this help you keep the keys before they slip away.

Acknowledgments

To the survivors who let me glimpse the raw truth of loss and endurance — your strength is the backbone of this book. To the families who allowed me into their stories, thank you for trusting me with the parts of life that most would rather turn away from. And to the readers who understand that clarity often comes wrapped in pain, I honor you for walking through these pages with open eyes.

To my own family: thank you for being my anchor — for the loyalty that steadies me, the lessons that shape me, and the love that makes the weight of this work worth carrying.

Intangible Assets / Simple Options Series — Copyright © 2025 by Emory I. Gary Jr.

Table of Contents

Dedication..6

Acknowledgments 7

Author's Note 10

A Gathering...11

The First Door..13

Writing on the Door 15

The Empty Pockets...16

Writing on the Door 18

The Double Lock..19

Writing on the Door 21

The Probate Gate 22

The Court decides if the papers don't...24

The Ostrich Turn..25

Writing on the Door 27

The Dumpster Fire Stop 28

Writing on the Door 30

The Gambler's Alley..31

Writing on the Door 33

The "You Thought It Was Yours" Door 34

Writing on the Door 36

The Trauma Room...37

Writing on the Door 39

A Discussion...40

Intangible Assets / Simple Options Series — Copyright © 2025 by Emory I. Gary Jr.

Who Kept the Keys?

About the Author 42
Discussion Guide 43

Intangible Assets / Simple Options Series — Copyright © 2025 by Emory I. Gary Jr.

Author's Note

This is a simple story.

It is meant to be read quickly, but remembered for a lifetime.

You will meet a few characters.

Some may remind you of someone you know.

Others may feel uncomfortably familiar.

The story is about The Keys—symbols of the things we all want to hold on to: our homes, our security, our peace of mind, and our future.

Like life itself, the story is short. But if you pay attention, you may see your own reflection in it.

And if you do, I hope you find a way to keep your keys.

Intangible Assets / Simple Options Series — Copyright © 2025 by Emory I. Gary Jr.

A Gathering

A small group of friends met one evening.

They had not been together in years. Each had taken a different path in life—different jobs, families, and fortunes.

At first they laughed about old times. But soon their talk grew serious.

One spoke of losing a husband.

Another described the long days after a mother's funeral.

A third admitted he worried about what his family would face if something happened to him tomorrow.

The room grew quiet.

Finally, one of them leaned forward.

"I know a story," she said.

"It's about The Keys. And how some people manage to keep them, while others lose them when it matters most."

Who Kept the Keys?

The others looked at her with curiosity.

"Tell us," they said.

And so she began…

Intangible Assets / Simple Options Series — Copyright © 2025 by Emory I. Gary Jr.

Who Kept the Keys?

The First Door

There were four friends who lived in a village not far from here.

Their names were Sam, Ray, Lynn, and Dee.

Every day they walked along the Path of Life, carrying their Keys. The Keys opened the doors to the things they wanted most: a home, safety, peace of mind, and a future for their families.

At first, the doors opened easily. They were young, healthy, and full of energy. The Path seemed simple, and the Keys seemed strong.

But as they walked further, things began to change. Some doors felt heavier. Some locks were harder to turn. And sometimes, the Keys they thought they held were not the ones they needed.

Sam noticed it first. "These doors won't always stay open," he said. "We should keep track of our Keys."

But Ray laughed. "We've always had them. Why worry now?"

Who Kept the Keys?

Lynn frowned, uncertain. And Dee only shrugged. "I'll deal with it later."

So the four friends kept walking. And soon, they came to the first door that would test them.

Writing on the Door

The Path always changes. The Keys must change with it.

Intangible Assets / Simple Options Series — Copyright © 2025 by Emory I. Gary Jr.

The Empty Pockets

The four friends came to a tall, dark door.

A sign above it read: "The End of a Journey."

They pushed it open and stepped inside. The room was quiet, lined with chairs and flowers. At the center stood a table where a family sat in silence.

On the table lay a piece of paper. It was a bill.

The family leaned over it, their faces pale. "It costs this much?" one of them whispered. "Eleven thousand..." another said, shaking their head. They looked at each other in disbelief.

Sam tightened his grip on his Keys. He understood. This was the cost of saying goodbye.

Ray frowned. "I didn't know it would be this high." Lynn glanced down at her hands. "I thought the Keys we had would cover it." Dee laughed nervously. "Maybe they'll figure it out somehow. That's not our problem."

Who Kept the Keys?

But as they watched, the family searched their pockets. Some pockets were empty. Others held only a few worn coins. They could not pay the bill in front of them.

Sam whispered, "This is what happens when the Keys aren't ready." Ray shook his head, unwilling to believe. Lynn shivered, uncertain of what it meant for her own future. And Dee turned away, pretending not to see.

When they left the room, the sound of that family's silence followed them down the Path.

Intangible Assets / Simple Options Series — Copyright © 2025 by Emory I. Gary Jr.

Who Kept the Keys?

Writing on the Door
A Key not prepared is a bill unpaid.

If you wait until the end, the cost will be higher.

Intangible Assets / Simple Options Series — Copyright © 2025 by Emory I. Gary Jr.

The Double Lock

Not far down the Path, the four friends reached another door.

It looked simple enough, with a single lock in the middle. But when Sam tried his Key, it turned only halfway. The door rattled, but it would not open.

"There must be another lock," Sam said.

Sure enough, just below the first was a second lock—hidden in the shadow, waiting.

Ray groaned. "One lock should have been enough." Lynn sighed. "We didn't plan for two." Dee laughed. "Maybe the first one was just for show. Try again."

But no matter how they tried, the first Key could not open the second lock.

Behind the door, they heard voices. A family sat with a man in a dark suit.

Who Kept the Keys?

"This is for the funeral," he said, pointing to one paper. "And this is for the burial," he added, laying down another. "They are separate. Always."

The family blinked in confusion. "We thought we had taken care of it already," one whispered. The man shook his head. "This is how it works. One bill does not pay the other."

The friends stepped back from the door.

Sam held his Keys tightly. "We have to be ready for both." Ray muttered, "No one told us this." Lynn nodded slowly, realizing the truth. And Dee walked on quickly, hoping the locks would disappear before she reached them again.

The Path grew narrower. The doors were getting harder to open.

Intangible Assets / Simple Options Series — Copyright © 2025 by Emory I. Gary Jr.

Writing on the Door
One door can hide another lock.

Two bills always follow one goodbye.

The Probate Gate

The Path led the four friends to a tall iron gate. It was heavier than any door they had seen before. Across the top, carved in stone, were the words: "The Court Decides."

Ray stepped forward with confidence. "These Keys are mine," he said. "I earned them. I know this gate will open for me."

He slid a Key into the lock and turned it hard. The gate groaned but did not move.

Sam tried next. His Key slipped in but stopped short, as though something unseen held it back.

From behind the bars, a voice spoke: "The Keys are not yours until the Court says so."

A man in a long coat stepped forward. He carried papers stamped with heavy seals. "These say who holds the Keys," he told them. "Not promises. Not wishes. Not even family ties. Only what is written and filed."

Lynn's eyes widened. "So even if you live in the house… even if you've paid for years… the Keys might not be yours?"

Who Kept the Keys?

The man nodded. "If the name is not on the paper, the gate will not open."

Ray's face turned red. "That's not fair!" But the man only repeated, "The Court decides."

Dee sighed. "I don't want to think about gates. I'll just keep walking." She turned away, pretending the bars were not there.

Sam held his Keys close. "We have to be certain whose names are written." Lynn whispered, "Or else the Keys can slip through our hands."

The iron gate loomed behind them as they continued down the Path. Its warning stayed with them: not all Keys belong to the hands that hold them.

Intangible Assets / Simple Options Series — Copyright © 2025 by Emory I. Gary Jr.

Who Kept the Keys?

The Court decides if the papers don't.

What is not written is not yours.

Intangible Assets / Simple Options Series — Copyright © 2025 by Emory I. Gary Jr.

Who Kept the Keys?

The Ostrich Turn

The Path bent sharply, leading into a wide, dusty clearing. In the middle stood a crossroads marked by a single post. On it hung a sign: "Face It or Ignore It."

The road to the left was straight but shadowed. The road to the right was bright but led nowhere.

Sam studied the sign. "We need to keep going, even if it's hard." Lynn nodded, uneasy but willing to follow.

Ray rubbed his chin. "Maybe if we wait, the shadows will clear."

Dee laughed. "I don't like shadows. I don't like signs. I don't like any of this."

Before anyone could stop her, she pulled a scarf from her pocket, wrapped it over her eyes, and sat down right at the post. "If I can't see it, it's not real," she said.

Sam frowned. "That won't make the Path go away." Lynn whispered, "If she waits here too long, she may never move

Intangible Assets / Simple Options Series — Copyright © 2025 by Emory I. Gary Jr.

again." Ray looked uneasy. "Maybe she's right. Maybe it will all work out."

But Sam shook his head. "Closing your eyes doesn't open doors. The Path keeps moving, whether you look at it or not."

They waited, but Dee would not rise. She tucked her head down like an ostrich in the sand and refused to face the road.

At last, Sam and Lynn moved forward, pulling Ray with them. They looked back once more, but Dee sat still at the crossroads, blindfolded by choice.

And the Path carried on without her.

Writing on the Door

Closing your eyes won't open doors.

Ignoring the Path does not stop it from moving.

The Dumpster Fire Stop

The Path grew narrow and steep. At the top of the hill, the friends saw smoke rising. They hurried forward and came to a small house, half-lit by fire. Flames licked from a barrel in the yard. Papers and clothes were scattered in the dirt.

A family ran back and forth, shouting, searching, clutching at scraps. Some tried to grab what they could. Others argued about what belonged to whom.

"This is mine!" one yelled. "No, it was promised to me!" another cried.

The fire burned brighter.

Sam whispered, "They lost their Keys." Lynn nodded. "Now they're fighting over ashes."

Ray stared, frozen. "This is what happens when no one plans…"

Dee was nowhere to be seen.

Intangible Assets / Simple Options Series — Copyright © 2025 by Emory I. Gary Jr.

Who Kept the Keys?

The family's voices rose in anger as the fire consumed what little remained.

Sam turned away. "Without the Keys, the Path becomes chaos."

The three friends walked on, the smoke clinging to their clothes as they left the scene behind.

Writing on the Door

Without the Keys, chaos takes over.

When no one plans, everyone loses.

Who Kept the Keys?

The Gambler's Alley

The Path led the friends into a narrow street lit by flickering lanterns. Above the doors hung signs painted in bright colors: "One More Chance." "Double or Nothing." "The House Always Wins."

Inside, voices shouted with excitement. Coins clattered across wooden tables. Cards slapped down in quick hands.

Sam stopped at the edge. "This isn't the way." But Ray stepped forward, his eyes wide. "Maybe we can win more Keys here. Maybe we can get ahead."

Lynn looked uncertain. "And if you lose?"

Ray shrugged. "We'll see." He tossed one of his Keys onto a table.

The dealer smiled, scooped it up, and set a card in front of him. Ray played, lost, and tried again. Another Key was taken. And another.

Sam shook his head. "You can't gamble with the Keys. They are meant to be guarded, not risked."

Who Kept the Keys?

The dealer leaned back with a grin. "The House always wins," he said, dropping Ray's last Key into a box.

Ray staggered back, his hands empty. His face was pale, his pockets bare.

Lynn whispered, "The Path is not a game." Sam answered softly, "Yet many play it as if it were."

They left the alley. Behind them, the laughter of the House echoed in the dark.

Intangible Assets / Simple Options Series — Copyright © 2025 by Emory I. Gary Jr.

Who Kept the Keys?

Writing on the Door
The House always wins when you risk your Keys.

You cannot bet tomorrow with today's Keys.

Intangible Assets / Simple Options Series — Copyright © 2025 by Emory I. Gary Jr.

Who Kept the Keys?

The "You Thought It Was Yours" Door

The Path grew quiet as the friends reached a heavy wooden door. Across the top were carved the words: "Ownership."

Ray, still shaken from his losses, hurried forward. "At least this one will open for me," he said. He pushed his Key into the lock and smiled as it turned.

But when the door swung open, another figure stepped out. A woman carried a paper in her hand. On it was a single line of writing.

"This says the Key is mine," she told Ray.

Ray stared at her in disbelief. "But I worked for it. I paid for it. Everyone knows it belongs to me."

The woman shook her head. "It doesn't matter what was promised. It matters what was written down."

Sam lowered his voice. "This is the danger. You can think the Key is yours… but if your name is not on the paper, it belongs to someone else."

Intangible Assets / Simple Options Series — Copyright © 2025 by Emory I. Gary Jr.

Who Kept the Keys?

Lynn's eyes filled with worry. "How many families have stood at this door, shocked when it opened for another?"

Ray clenched his fists. "It isn't fair!" he cried.

But the woman only held up the paper once more, turned, and walked away with the Key.

The door closed, leaving Ray empty-handed.

Sam whispered, "The Path teaches us, again and again: the Keys go to those whose names are written."

They moved on, the weight of the lesson pressing against them like the locked door behind.

Intangible Assets / Simple Options Series — Copyright © 2025 by Emory I. Gary Jr.

Writing on the Door
What isn't written isn't yours.

A promise is not a Key.

The Trauma Room

The Path ended at a silent building. Its doors were wide and cold, the kind that seemed to open only one way.

Inside, the walls were bare. At the center of the room stood a single table, covered with papers, locks, and broken Keys.

A family sat around it, their faces pale with shock. They held the pieces of Keys that no longer fit any door. Some cried. Some argued. Others sat in silence, too tired to speak.

Sam whispered, "This is what happens when the Keys are left until it is too late."

Lynn looked closer. "These Keys were strong once. But without care, they cracked. And now nothing opens for them."

Ray stepped forward, his hands still empty. He saw his own reflection in the broken metal. "I thought I had time," he said softly. "But the Path does not wait."

No one answered. The room itself seemed to speak the truth: The Keys had been lost. The doors were closed.

Intangible Assets / Simple Options Series — Copyright © 2025 by Emory I. Gary Jr.

Who Kept the Keys?

The three friends left quietly. Behind them, the Trauma Room stood as a warning to all who would walk the Path unprepared.

Intangible Assets / Simple Options Series — Copyright © 2025 by Emory I. Gary Jr.

Writing on the Door
Broken Keys open nothing.

The Path does not wait for those who delay.

Intangible Assets / Simple Options Series — Copyright © 2025 by Emory I. Gary Jr.

Who Kept the Keys?

A Discussion

The story ends.

For a moment, the room was still. The friends who had gathered leaned back in their chairs, each lost in thought.

Finally, someone broke the silence. "I saw myself in Ray," he admitted. "I've been waiting, hoping things will work out. But now I know I could lose the Keys if I don't act."

Another spoke up. "I've done what Dee did. I've looked away. I told myself I'd deal with it later. But the Path keeps moving. I can't sit at the crossroads forever."

A third shook her head slowly. "The Probate Gate frightened me most. I thought my family was safe. But the Court decides unless the papers are clear. I can't leave that to chance."

They all turned to the woman who had told the story. "You've made your point," one said. "The Keys matter. If we don't prepare, we lose them."

She nodded. "It's never too early to prepare. But it can be too late."

Intangible Assets / Simple Options Series — Copyright © 2025 by Emory I. Gary Jr.

Who Kept the Keys?

Intangible Assets / Simple Options Series — Copyright © 2025 by Emory I. Gary Jr.

About the Author

Emory I. Gary Jr. has spent years walking alongside families during some of life's hardest transitions. Through his work, his teaching, and his own lived experience, he has seen the difference between those who prepare and those who do not. This story was written not just to be read, but to be used—a guide to help people hold on to the things that matter most when the Path grows difficult.

He lives with his family in Georgia, where he continues to write, teach, and help others prepare for the doors they will one day face.

Intangible Assets / Simple Options Series — Copyright © 2025 by Emory I. Gary Jr.

Who Kept the Keys?

Discussion Guide

This story is short, but its lessons can last a lifetime. Use these questions to reflect on your own Keys—or to guide a group discussion.

1. Which character did you relate to most—Sam, Ray, Lynn, or Dee? Why?

2. Which Door in the story felt most familiar to you? The Empty Pockets? The Double Lock? The Probate Gate? The Ostrich Turn? The Dumpster Fire Stop? The Gambler's Alley? The "You Thought It Was Yours" Door? The Trauma Room?

3. Have you ever felt like you lost a Key? What happened?

4. What Keys do you still hold today? Are you confident they will open the doors you will face?

5. What could you do now to make sure your Keys are safe in the future?

6. How could this story help someone you know who may not be prepared?

Intangible Assets / Simple Options Series — Copyright © 2025 by Emory I. Gary Jr.

Who Kept the Keys?

Remember: the Path keeps moving forward.

The doors will appear, whether you are ready or not.

The only question is:

Will you keep the Keys?

Intangible Assets / Simple Options Series — Copyright © 2025 by Emory I. Gary Jr.

Who Kept the Keys?

End of Book

Intangible Assets / Simple Options Series — Copyright © 2025 by Emory I. Gary Jr.

www.ingramcontent.com/pod-product-compliance
Lightning Source LLC
Chambersburg PA
CBHW070042070426
42449CB00012BA/3141